MW00888199

FATHER'S DAY FIRE PLAN

A Guide to Preventing House Fires and Keeping Your Family Safe

by Robert Wittenberg

illustrations by Michelle Bloemers

Although the author has made every effort to ensure that the information in this book was correct at the time of publishing, the author does not assume and hereby disclaims any liability to any party for any loss, damage, or disruption caused by errors or omissions, whether from negligence, accident, or any other cause.

While the steps recommended in this book are intended to reduce the risk of injury or death in a fire, there are no guarantees of survival in an emergency.

Copyright © 2020 by Robert Wittenberg

All rights reserved.

Independently published

ISBN: 9798646176197

TABLE OF CONTENTS

INTRODUCTION

My wife and I have raised three children together and they have all grown into amazing people. They are funny, smart, compassionate, creative, and brave. They laugh at each other often and even more so, at themselves. They are the kind of people that I wish I could be, and I couldn't imagine my life without them.

When they were younger, we followed all of the safety recommendations that we could. We placed them securely in their car seats and made sure they were always protected with baby gates inside of our home. They rode with bike helmets and learned to drive with their cell phones in the back seat. We did the things we knew would keep them safe.

This was a very different experience from when I was growing up. When I was a kid, we would pile into the back of pickup trucks. We would make bike jumps out of scrap materials and set them up in the middle of the street. We played outside well past dark and only came home when dinner was ready. It's not that we were especially brave, it was just nobody thought it was unsafe.

And it's not that I didn't get hurt either. In fact, I was constantly healing from some form of an injury. I always had scraped knees and banged up elbows from skateboarding. I once punctured my foot with a pitchfork, trying to be funny. I fractured my cheekbone while learning how to ski. I cut my arm with a chainsaw when I wasn't paying attention. These scars were just trophies of my adventurous life, and I was proud of them.

As a father, I took a completely different approach to safety and thought I was doing everything I could to keep my kids safe.

One night, however, the smoke alarm in the upstairs hallway went off, and nobody else woke up. I jumped out of bed to investigate. Luckily, there was no fire, but I wasn't sure why the alarm went off in the first place. It was in that moment that I realized there was more I had to do in order to keep my family safe.

I needed to make sure my kids were able to recognize the sound of a smoke alarm if they heard it, and if one went off in the middle of the night again, I wanted to be sure they would know what it was, and, more importantly, what to do.

I started by having the kids help me change the batteries in each of the smoke alarms twice a year. It became sort of a game for us. We would start by first tracking down each smoke alarm, one by one. I would reach up and twist the unit off its ceiling mount, while the kids stood ready to help.

One of them would take the old batteries from me, while another handed me the new ones. Whoever was last would then press the test button. They would cover their ears and scream after hearing how loud it was. I felt better that they were now aware and had an active part in helping to keep our home safe.

When I became a professional home inspector in 2006, I began to learn more about new safety recommendations that I had never even considered before, including the use of carbon monoxide alarms, the importance of maintaining heating systems, and cleaning your chimney flues. Even though I was presenting clear and easy to follow safety recommendations that would help protect my clients' families, I was still not sharing all of these recommendations with my own family.

In 2012, I became a volunteer firefighter and EMT because I wanted to give back to my community. The experience gave me the opportunity to work with some amazing people who taught me the importance of volunteering. I learned from dedicated, professional firefighters who opened my eyes to the people who are in need and the type of person it takes to always be ready to help. I learned that with great training, preparation, and the right tools, you can solve just about any problem.

I also learned how house fires start and spread and how quickly conditions can become deadly. It wasn't long before I realized I needed to do more for my own family. Even with access to all sorts of community awareness programs and just as many other articles sharing fire safety tips, I was still missing one thing: using all that information and turning it into an action plan.

Until, a few years ago, my kids asked me what I wanted to do for Father's Day. I decided that all I wanted was a few hours of their time to create and practice our own family fire plan.

The best part of this idea was including everyone in the family – my wife and all three kids. I knew I couldn't protect my kids from everything myself but if I could include them in planning, they would learn how to protect themselves in case of a fire. They would find a way to get outside safely on their own.

On that Father's Day, we spent a few hours talking about where fires may start in a home and how a fire would most likely spread. We sounded the smoke alarms and talked about what to do if they went off again. We discussed the importance of staying low to the ground and feeling the doors for heat before opening them. We looked around each room and discovered other ways we could get out, if the door was hot and blocked by flames. We climbed out of each window and found a path we could use to reconnect at the end of the driveway. Together, we worked through each decision that needed to be made in order for us to get out of the house safely.

The kids came up with some really tough questions, too. What if everyone doesn't get out of the house in time? What about our dog and cat, how were they supposed to get out? How do we get help from our neighbors? No matter how important the questions were, we certainly didn't have all of the answers, but at least we finally started the conversation.

This is where the idea for *Father's Day Fire Plan* was born. I wanted to take a specific day, one that is already dedicated to celebrating fatherhood and the importance of family, and make the time to work through a fire plan, together. To talk about how we, as a family, can strive to prevent fires, but also how to respond quickly and safely, if one does occur.

My goal for this book is to provide you and your family with simple steps that can be started now, to reduce the risk of fires in your home. I also hope to help you build a plan that will fit your family perfectly and one that will allow you to get everyone out safely. I've learned that so many things within a home change drastically over the years, and that making an updated, and quick, evacuation plan is more important than ever.

This book is meant for everyone: dads, moms, grandparents, aunts, uncles, kids, and family friends, to encourage families to work together in creating a fire safety plan that will protect everyone in the home.

Any day you pick to dedicate to home safety is great. It does not have to be Father's Day. It can be Mother's Day, a child's birthday, an anniversary, the day you bought your first house, or the first day of any month. The most important thing is simply finding a day that everyone will be able to commit themselves to creating a solid safety plan.

For me, it was all about just starting the conversation, so let's get started.

THE THREE BEHAVIORS

The first step in creating a family fire plan is to understand three important behaviors that directly affect residential structure fires: the behavior of fire itself, the behavior of structures when burning, and the behavior of people in an emergency.

Being able to understand these behaviors, and how they have changed in recent years, is critical to understand why it is more important than ever to have a practiced family fire plan.

To begin, the way that fire behaves is dependent on the available fuel, oxygen, and heat within a space. When we reduce or eliminate any of those three components, we are able to slow the spread of fire and eventually control it.

However, the speed and intensity of fire growth has changed significantly in recent years, due to the extensive use of synthetic fabric and wood materials in home furnishings.

This has greatly reduced the time available to exit before the home becomes inhabitable.

Secondly, the physical structure of a home can not only influence a fire's growth but also how it behaves while it's burning. Homes have changed drastically over the years, in a variety of ways. New design trends, light weight material use, and different construction methods have drastically increased the speed at which fire spreads throughout a home. This has led to faster structural failure, and, therefore, less time for evacuation.

Lastly, how people respond during an emergency situation is greatly influenced by their own preparedness and knowledge of the building they are in. Even though human behavior in emergency situations may be somewhat predictable, we can still influence how well people will respond by increasing their awareness of their environment and the building's layout.

CHAPTER 1 – THE BASICS OF FIRE BEHAVIOR

To understand the dangers of structure fires, we will begin with how fire behaves, identifying it's needs and weaknesses, recognizing how it feeds itself, and lastly, how it spreads throughout a space.

We will also discuss how fire behavior has changed over the last few decades and, as a result of newer engineered materials and changes in construction methods, burns faster and hotter than ever before.

Simply put, fire is the rapid decomposition of a material. When materials are exposed to extreme heat, they begin to break down, or decompose, quickly. When a material is burning, its mass is converted into energy in the form of heat and light. This process is not perfect; unfortunately, smoke, soot, ash, and toxic gases are common byproducts of combustion, further adding to the dangers of a fire.

Fire has three basic components that allow it to continue burning: sufficient fuel, sufficient heat, and sufficient oxygen. This is called the Fire Triangle.

Since fire relies so heavily on these three components, they also become fire's weaknesses. Remove any one – fuel, heat, or oxygen – and the burning process slows and eventually stops. For example, a campfire will ultimately go out when we stop adding firewood to it. Or if it rains on that same campfire, the rain water will absorb the campfire's heat, and the fire will go out. Or if

THE FIRE TRIANGLE

we shovel sand onto the fire, we remove its oxygen supply, and the fire will go out.

Common Classes of Fuels

The best way to put out a fire is dependent on the type of fuel that is burning. The most common fuels in residential fires are divided into three types.

Class A fuels include common household materials, more specifically, wood, paper, and fabric. This class of fire is generally extinguished by cooling the fuel with water or a multi-purpose fire extinguisher.

Class B fuels include flammable liquids and gases, such as gasoline, kerosene, paints and oils, and cleaning products. These fires can be extinguished by separating the oxygen from the fuel with a multi-purpose fire extinguisher.

Class C fuels involve energized electrical appliances and/or electrical wiring. Using water, or other conductive extinguishing agents, can be highly dangerous. These types of fires are best fought with a non-conductive, multi-purpose fire extinguisher.

Commonly found multi-purpose fire extinguishers that are rated ABC can be used on any of the three classes of residential fires. They are made with non-conductive monoammonium phosphate. To maximize safety, these multi-purpose fire extinguishers should be located in the kitchen, laundry room, and garage. We will discuss more about fire extinguishers and their use in a later chapter.

Methods of Heat Transfer

When materials are heated to their ignition temperature, they will ignite and begin to transfer heat to other materials nearby. Heat transfers by one of three methods:

CONDUCTION

Conduction: Direct contact between materials allows heat to efficiently transfer from one item to the next. Think about a skillet heating up on an electric stove.

CONVECTION

Convection: As heat rises, materials that are above the burning matter are heated, without ever coming in direct contact with the fuel. This is like when you place your hand above a candle or when you roast a marshmallow for smores.

Radiation: Heat energy is radiated outward in every direction, heating materials without direct contact with the fuel. For example, you can feel the heat from a fireplace from across the room.

RADIATION

House fires can start and spread through any or all of these heat transfer methods.

Fire Growth

As heat transfers from one material to another, fire spreads, further increasing the amount of heat, smoke, and toxic gases that will fill the room quickly.

Under these conditions, it is difficult for humans to survive. It would only take a few seconds of breathing superheated smoke and toxic gases to sear our throat and lung tissues, causing fatal asphyxiation. According to a 2011 National Fire Protection Association (NFPA) study, 75% of the home fire deaths between 1999 and 2008 were directly related to smoke inhalation.[1]

As heat continues to increase within a confined space, furnishings, draperies, and carpeting can all be brought to their ignition temperature quickly. When all materials within the space reach their ignition temperature and ignite simultaneously, this is called a flashover. When a room reaches the flashover stage, it immediately becomes unsurvivable for people.

Changes in Fire Behavior Due to Synthetic Materials

The speed of fire growth and the rate at which people and structures are impacted have increased significantly due to the materials we use to furnish our homes now.

Prior to the 1950s, home furnishings were predominantly made up of natural materials, such as solid woods, leather, wool, and natural cotton fabrics. These items were slow to ignite and slow to burn.

However, changes in furniture design and production, as well as an increase in demand and broader retail availability, have introduced newer home furnishings that include synthetic materials and adhesives. Upholstered items, such as couches, chairs, and mattresses, are padded with polyurethane foam and covered with other synthetic fabrics, including polyester and nylon.

Solid wood items, like tables, bookcases, dressers, and other forms of cabinetry, are now produced using wood composite materials. These materials include adhesives, resins, and other laminated wood products.

Additionally, it has become more popular for furniture and other items to be produced with plastic materials.

Using these engineered materials has a positive environmental benefit, including reducing the use and waste of natural materials, while also making the production, shipping, and ownership of these products more cost effective for the manufacturer and the consumer.

Unfortunately, the switch from natural materials to synthetic materials has drastically increased the rate of fire growth and toxicity. These synthetic and engineered materials burn hotter and produce more toxic gases, including hydrogen cyanide and carbon monoxide. These new conditions have greatly decreased the survival time in a fire.

In 2012, an Underwriters Laboratories study examined the change in fire behavior within rooms that contained modern furnishings versus similar rooms, with older furnishings.[2] The tests calculated the speed of reaching flashover in both rooms, measuring the difference between traditional and synthetic materials, as well as construction techniques. The results were devastating.

During the experiment, six rooms were built to compare the reaction differences. Four rooms were built with dimensions commonly found in older home designs, with each room being approximately 12 feet by 12 feet, for a total of 144 square feet.

An additional pair of rooms were built larger and more consistent with open concept spaces, which is the layout preferred today. Each room was approximately 13 feet by 18 feet, for a total of 234 square feet.

All of the rooms had furnishings that were placed in similar orientations. Three of the rooms had older, legacy furnishings with fabrics using natural materials, while the other three had new modern furnishings using synthetic materials and engineered wood.

In each of the rooms, a burning candle was placed in the corner of the sofa and was allowed to continue to ignite the room until the point of flashover occurred.

In the two smaller rooms with the older, natural fabric and solid wood furnishings, the time it took to reach flashover was approximately 30 minutes. In the third, larger room with older materials, the fire involved the couch and curtains but actually failed to reach flashover at all and eventually self-extinguished.

A time to flashover that approaches 30 minutes would likely provide sufficient time for an alarm to activate and for all of the residents to get outside safely. However, in the rooms with newer materials, the times were significantly less and would likely not allow for someone to get out safely.

The first smaller room with new furnishings transitioned to flashover in only 3 minutes and 40 seconds. The second room hit flashover at 4 minutes and 45 seconds, and the third room, with a larger space, hit flashover in 3 minutes and 20 seconds.

The Key Lesson about Modern Fire Behavior

Modern furnishings have greatly reduced the possibility for escape by decreasing the evacuation time from the moment a fire first ignites, from approximately 30 minutes to less than three. This eliminates most of the time we have to recognize that a fire exists, respond to it appropriately, and get everyone out of the house safely.

CHAPTER 2 – THE BASICS OF STRUCTURAL BEHAVIOR

Cultural influences, climate conditions, availability of materials, durability requirements, and design aesthetics have changed home design significantly over time. Other changes were made to add functional needs like electrical and plumbing systems.

Recent mandates for greater energy efficiency and consumer demand for open concept spaces with higher ceiling heights have drastically impacted fire behavior in our modern homes.

While energy efficiency continues to improve in heating and cooling systems, appliances, and lighting, the primary focus of the construction industry has been on enhancing insulation and reducing the air exchange between the interior and the exterior. We have gained greater energy efficiency by increasing wall, floor, and attic insulation levels, as well as sealing gaps around windows, doors, and other exterior wall penetrations. Even though these improvements prevent heat loss during cooler months and heat infiltration during warmer months, they also increase the retention of heat and smoke inside the house, speeding up the time to flashover in the event of a fire.

Secondly, the increase in consumer demand for open floor plans with higher ceiling heights has created larger interior spaces. Smaller rooms with standard ceiling heights would naturally limit the number of belongings that immediately become a part of any fire. Fires could be contained to kitchens, dining rooms, family rooms, or living rooms. With larger open rooms, there is extra oxygen and fuel, significantly increasing the fire's temperature and smoke production.

The Effect of Engineered Structural Wood.

Lastly, to reduce construction costs and time, today's homes are built with engineered wood products, such as wood trusses, engineered I-joists, oriented strand board (OSB) sheets, and laminated wood beams. These products are specifically engineered to be stronger than traditional lumber and can span longer distances without sagging. They are also effective in reducing the time required to frame a home.

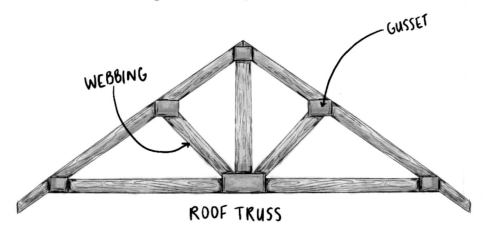

ROOF TRUSS

Wood trusses utilize 2'x4' or 2'x6' wood, secured together with metal plates, called gusset plates. Trusses are used in place of traditional lumber to support roof and floor structures. Engineered I-joists are assembled using laminated strips of wood and OSB sheeting to support floors and roofs. Their design allows them to span greater distances than that of traditional lumber. Oriented Strand Board (OSB) uses smaller pieces of wood, glued together, to form sheets similar to plywood. Laminated wood beams also use smaller pieces of lumber, glued together to form larger beams.

These engineered wood products are designed to create lighter and stronger structural components, at a more cost-effective price, and with lower environmental impact.

However, they have also been shown to burn faster and reach a point of structural failure in a fraction of the time of traditional lumber products. An Underwriters Lab study showed that older, traditional dimensional lumber floor joists fail in 30 to 45 minutes, compared to newer engineered wood floor joists that fail in 6 minutes, under similar conditions.[3]

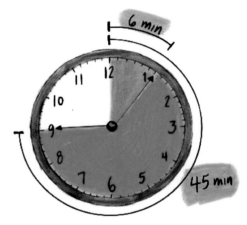

The Key Lesson about Engineered Wood Materials

The speed at which a fire spreads within a home has changed dramatically over the last few decades, due to the alterations in construction design, energy efficiency, and the prevalence of synthetic materials in home furnishings. New designs and floor plans allow for more rapid fire and smoke spread, higher levels of heat retention, and shorter times to structural failure.

These changes significantly decrease the amount of time available to safely get out of a home, in case of fire. The need for quick response and egress is now more critical than ever, as a well-practiced plan for rapid evacuation is the most effective method for increasing survival, in case of a fire.

CHAPTER 3 - THE BASICS OF HUMAN BEHAVIOR

I f your workplace is like mine, fire alarms are more of a nuisance than anything, since they get tested so often. When the alarm goes off, everyone in my office keeps working, despite the sound. This is a relatively common response that has been substantiated in a number of studies.

According to the National Institute of Standards and Technology (NIST), occupants in commercial buildings were found to consistently disregard fire alarms until they received confirmation from a trusted source, or actually smelled or saw smoke and/or flames.[4]

How people respond in a fire is dependent, among other things, on their own awareness and familiarity with the building they are in. For example, an evaluation of the deadly Station Nightclub fire in 2003 showed that after becoming aware of the fire, a great majority of the occupants moved toward the familiar front entrance, rather than any other exits. Despite being clearly marked, other exits were not familiar to the occupants and were not utilized as much as the entrance that they came in.[5]

While most studies tend to focus on commercial or workplace responses, others illustrate predictable human behavior in home fires. Most importantly, they show that we can actually influence the behaviors of those in our family by initiating early communication. Talking about an emergency before it happens and what to do during one can increase the knowledge and familiarity of other evacuation options.

Imagine a smoke alarm suddenly sounds in your home. As parents, you are likely the first to investigate. This is where your confirmation of the alarm as a trusted source is important. If a fire condition is found, yelling to others in your family is more effective in initiating an evacuation than an individual alarm. Remember though, this responsibility does not need to be the parent's alone. If children are empowered to notify others in the family, they can feel more in control and have a share in securing the family's safety.

Making family members aware and comfortable with all of the available exits, more than just the front entry door, will increase their ability to quickly identify all of the ways out in an emergency. For example, if the front door is blocked, making a path toward a back or side door may not be difficult to imagine if someone has done it before. Or, if a bedroom door is blocked and exiting out of the window is familiar, it will more likely be utilized in an emergency situation.

This is why practicing an escape plan is incredibly beneficial. As we will discuss in later chapters, practicing the actual process of climbing out of a window and making a path toward the front of the home makes it much more likely to be used in an emergency.

With smaller children, there is an added behavior that can have a significant effect on their survival. A child's first response may be to hide when facing something scary. This can include turning away from strangers, tucking their face into a parent, or by hiding under a bed or in a closet. If they can't see what is scaring them, then they may feel they are safe. In a fire situation, they may choose to hide under their bed covers, in a closet, under the bed, or anywhere else that will make them feel protected.

The need to hide may be more intense if the child feels somehow responsible for starting the fire.

Firefighters search thoroughly when seeking out a possible victim but intentionally hiding makes any child harder to find. Besides being afraid of the fire, adding to a child's fear is now strangers, donned in full protective gear, presenting them with a rather ominous silhouette.

To reduce the fear of firefighters, I recommend visiting your local fire station or taking advantage of community events where the fire department is available. These events allow kids to see firefighters up close with their protective bunker gear, air tanks, masks, and tools, while in a far less threatening environment. Once children see the firefighter inside their protective shell in this setting, they are more likely to believe that firefighters are not something to fear but instead someone who is there to help.

One concept that is constantly reinforced in fire service training, and something that I try to work on whenever I am someplace new, is maintaining situational awareness. Situational awareness means having an awareness of the conditions that you find yourself in, recognizing any hazards before they emerge, and anticipating possible pathways to safety. This also includes an honest awareness of your own physical capabilities, including your strength and skills, as well as tools and other resources that are available to you, if needed.

Becoming more aware of your surroundings, wherever you are in everyday life, can significantly affect your response in a hazardous or emergency situation. Try identifying the closest exit in a movie theater before the lights dim, walking the path to the closest emergency exit from your hotel room, or even recognizing the different directions out of your stadium seat, whether behind you, in front of you, or to the sides. Becoming familiar with multiple exits will not only give you more options when everyone else is crowding the main exit but also a sense of confidence in evacuating, when conditions turn deadly.

Having situational awareness in private places is just as important as it is in public. When visiting someone in their home or staying in a new place, identifying exits will improve your chances of getting out safely.

In any location, it is also important to recognize how you can guide those that are with you to the best exit as well. This may involve pointing out the exits to children, sitting on the aisle if seating allows, and/or talking about the way out beforehand, if conditions become dangerous.

The Key Lessons about Influencing Family Behavior

This understanding presents important steps for improving behavior in the event of an emergency:

First, empowering everyone in the family to loudly call out when fire conditions are discovered will give everyone a greater sense of control over the household's safety. Make sure to let kids know that they, too, have the ability to alert others in the home when necessary.

Secondly, improving familiarity of primary and secondary exits in your home, from all rooms, will make it easier to consider every option when looking to exit quickly.

Thirdly, awareness can reduce a child's fear in emergency situations. Taking the opportunity to expose them to firefighting equipment, including full turnout gear, can also increase familiarity and reduce their fear.

Lastly, making efforts to increase your situational awareness whenever in new or unfamiliar places, can increase your ability to respond quickly.

How people behave in emergency situations may not always be totally predictable, but having a plan and preparing beforehand, may improve behavior and provide the best possible outcome.

PREVENT, PLAN, & PRACTICE

As mentioned earlier, there are three important behaviors that affect the intensity and survivability of structure fires.

With some additional knowledge, we can also take a number of steps to reduce the risk of fires occurring in the home in the first place. Through planning and practicing, we can improve how each of us react to an emergency situation and increase our ability to get out quickly.

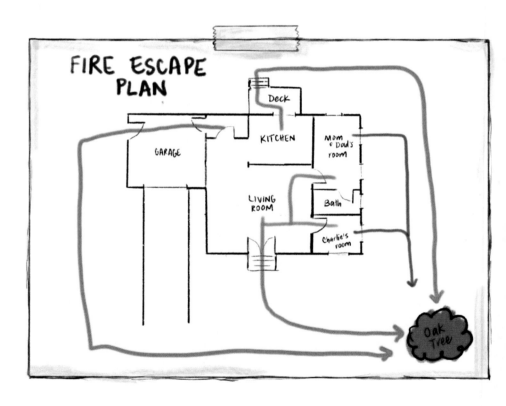

CHAPTER 4 - COMMON HOUSEHOLD FIRE DANGERS

I n the previous chapters, we discussed how modern construction materials and techniques, as well as modern home design and its furnishings, have decreased the time between fire ignition and unsurvivable flashover.

We also learned that how people behave in an emergency situation is predictable and can be influenced through communication and awareness.

With both of those things in mind, it should still be understood that the best method for preventing dangerous house fires is to keep smaller fires from starting in the first place.

Now, let's talk about some of the most common areas that fires can start in your home and some simple ways to reduce those risks.

Kitchen Safety

Most home fires start in the kitchen for the simple reason that this is where we do the cooking.

Fires that begin while cooking are typically due to one of two main causes: Overheated food, grease or cooking oils, or flammable materials coming into contact with burners.

Here are a few steps you can take to prevent kitchen fires:

Do not leave the kitchen unattended when cooking. Pay attention to what you are doing, especially when frying, grilling, boiling, and broiling. Unattended cooking is the leading cause of fires in the kitchen.

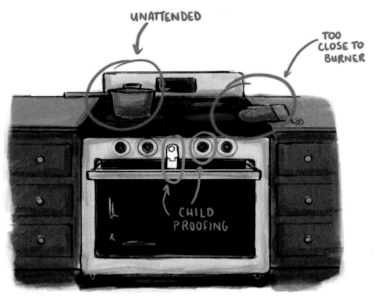

Keep flammable materials away from burners. This includes dishcloths, oven mitts, paper towels, cookbooks, and any other flammable materials. When cooking, avoid wearing long sleeves that hang down and can ignite when reaching back to the rear burners.

Install proper childproofing devices. With young children in the home, proper childproofing should be installed to prevent unintended activation of burners. Safety devices include childproof knob covers on ranges and door locks on oven doors.

Know how to respond to small cooktop fires. If a fire occurs in a pan when cooking, turn off the burner and carefully slide a lid over the top of the pan. Never try to move a pan with burning material to the sink. You risk spreading the burning material across the kitchen and increase the risk of burning yourself if you do so.

Know how to respond to oven fires. If a fire occurs when baking or roasting in the oven, turn off the oven and keep the oven door closed. This removes the heat source and limits the oxygen available to the fire. It should then burn out on its own.

Keep a multi-purpose fire extinguisher in the kitchen. Larger cooking fires and grease fires can be extinguished with a multipurpose fire extinguisher. Multipurpose extinguishers will have an ABC or BC rating.

ABC EXTINGUISHER

Fireplace and Chimney Safety

Unintended fireplace fires may result when flammable materials escape the fireplace opening or flammable materials come too close to the fireplace opening. Chimney fires occur when accumulated residues or other obstructions in the chimney flue ignite. These types of fires are preventable, as well.

When using a wood burning fireplace, extra care should be taken to keep burning fuel inside the fireplace, as well as making sure all belongings are kept away from the firebox opening. The use of a properly sized fireplace screen will contain fire embers, keeping flammable materials off the hearth and away from the fireplace opening will reduce the risk of ignition.

Chimney fires primarily occur due to the accumulation of creosote in the chimney flue. Creosote is a flammable mixture of oils, soot, and unburned fuel that adheres to the interior lining of a chimney flue. This can be formed by burning unseasoned firewood and/or providing insufficient combustion air.

Other chimney obstructions can also create fire and venting hazards, including animals and vegetation in the chimney flue. It is not unusual for animals to be attracted to the warmth of a chimney in the cooler months and fall into an open chimney flue or nest in an open chimney flue during the warmer months. Tree branches and falling leaves can also block proper venting of open chimney flues.

Here are a couple of steps you can take to prevent fireplace and chimney fire hazards:

Keep fuel loads small. Do not overfill fireplaces with excess wood or paper materials.

Use fireplace screens. These will keep burning materials and embers from escaping the interior firebox.

Keep flammable materials at least three feet away from any open fireplace. Keep the hearth clear of baskets, blankets, carpeting, and other flammable materials.

Do not leave the fireplace unattended. Burning logs can shift, allowing burning wood or embers to escape the firebox.

Have your fireplace and chimney inspected and cleaned yearly by a qualified chimney sweep. Chimney sweeps will remove any accumulated creosote, clear any blockages, evaluate and repair any structural weakness, and ensure proper and safe operation of the fireplace and chimney. The Chimney Safety Institute of America (www.csia.org) provides further information about fireplace and chimney maintenance and how to find a qualified chimney sweep in your area.

Check or install chimney caps. Also called spark arrestors, these devices prevent burning embers from escaping from the top of the chimney and can prevent animals from entering the chimney flue, as well. Chimney caps can be installed by a competent homeowner, a handyman, or a chimney sweep themselves. However, care should always be exercised when walking on roofs or working on ladders, at any height.

Garage Fire Safety

Garages are where we tend to store gasoline, paint, cleaners, and other flammable liquids, alongside boxes and other items we don't have room for inside. We also keep cars in the garage, along with the lawn mower, weed trimmer, and other gas-powered tools. Considering this, it may be unsurprising to learn garages are a very common place for fires to start.

Here are a couple of steps you can take to prevent garage fires:

Do not store damp rags in closed spaces. When using flammable liquids, make sure to hang any rags, brushes, or rollers in open space until they are fully dry before disposing.

Keep flammable liquids high up on a shelf or in a sealed cabinet. Flammable vapors are generally heavier than air and once released, they will settle along the floor. Any ignition source in the garage, such as a water heater, furnace or electrical outlet, runs the risk of igniting the newly settled vapor and causing a fire. Containing these vapors or separating the flammable liquid container from these vapors reduces the risk of ignition.

PREVENT, PLAN, & PRACTICE

Do not put gas powered tools away hot. Always allow lawn mowers, weed whackers, pressure washers, and other combustion engine tools to fully cool off before storing them in a closed garage.

Keep a multi-purpose fire extinguisher in the garage. Smaller fires can be extinguished with a multipurpose fire extinguisher, more specifically those with an ABC rating.

Maintain separation between the garage and the interior. Proper fire barriers should be installed and maintained to prevent a garage fire from quickly moving inside and into other parts of the home. This includes covering any openings in the wall between the garage and the interior, as well as any openings leading into the attic or crawl space. Additionally, the door between your garage and your interior should be fitted with self-closing hinges. Remember that, in order to keep a properly sealed fit, pet doors should not be installed in the door between the garage and the interior.

Electrical Safety

According to the NFPA, faulty or damaged electrical and appliance wiring was responsible for an average of 44,880 home structure fires each year between 2012 and 2016.[6] To understand how these types of fires occur, some electrical basics may be helpful.

Electricity flows through circuits running from the utility service pole to the breaker panel and then from the breaker panel to the electrical fixture or appliance. Electrical current flows through these circuits and then back to its source to complete its path. If the flow is interrupted in any manner (i.e. the breaker is tripped or turned off, the wall or appliance switch is turned off or the appliance is unplugged, etc.) the flow of electricity stops.

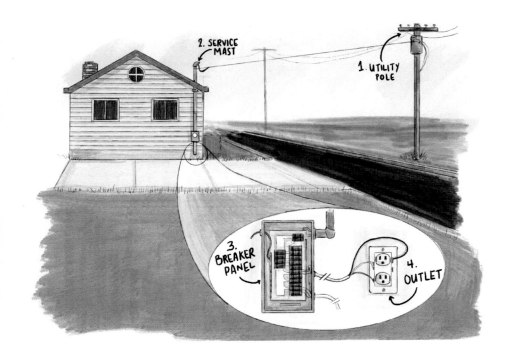

When electricity is properly contained within its circuit, it is safe. However, if it can find a secondary path through another conductive material, the current can flow outside the circuit. This creates opportunities for electrical shock, overheating, or ignition of flammable materials.

The amount of electrical current that flows through a circuit is measured in amps. The larger the diameter of the wiring, the more amps the wire can carry without overheating. When devices that draw more amps than a circuit is able to handle get plugged in, the circuit gets overloaded. When a circuit overloads, it overheats, which can melt the insulative covering and ignite flammable materials that come in contact with the wiring.

To reduce the risk of overloading circuits, breakers are installed to automatically shut off the circuit if the amperage exceeds what the breaker is rated for. When breakers trip, they interrupt the circuit, stopping the flow of electricity, thus preventing the wire from overheating.

Here are a number of things you can do to prevent electrical fires:

Reduce the use of extension cords. Extension cords are often used to connect multiple devices into a single outlet. However, extension cords are commonly overloaded with too many appliances and may overheat. Additionally, they may be more prone to damage from furniture, carpeting, and/or foot traffic. Lastly, they are usually hidden from view, increasing the risk of overheating without being noticed.  The use of extension cords should be eliminated or minimized as much as possible.

Do not overload outlets. With the increase in the number of devices that we have, the need for places to plug them in has also increased. Because most older homes do not have enough outlets to meet those needs, the use of power strips and multi plugs has become more popular. Often, a single receptacle will hold plugs to a multitude of devices, creating an overheating risk.

As much as possible, reduce the use of multi-outlet adapters and when their use is necessary, check these devices frequently for loose connections and overheating.

Check appliances for frayed cords. Older and overused appliance cords can become worn over time, breaking down the insulative covering and exposing the active wiring inside. This increases the risk of fire and shock hazards. Using electrical tape to wrap the damaged wiring is common but is not a long-term solution and should be discouraged. Any damaged cords should be completely replaced, as soon as possible.

Check for wiring that is warm to the touch. Wiring that is warm to the touch indicates overheating. This can include accessible wiring, as well as electrical outlets, switches, and dimmers. If wiring is found to be warm, the electrical load on that circuit or wire should be reduced. This can be done by decreasing fixtures or appliances using that circuit.

Get professional help. Have a qualified, licensed electrician inspect electrical panels, switches, outlets, and visible wiring for damage or overheating. Because assessment of these symptoms may only be visible behind outlet and switch cover plates or inside the main electrical panel, this should be completed by a qualified professional.

Heating System Safety

Common residential heating systems include: forced air systems that push air heated by fuel burning or electrical coils throughout ductwork in the home; radiant heat systems that distribute heated liquid through piping or by concealed electrical wiring; and electric heating systems with individual baseboard heaters or portable electrical heaters.

Fire concerns relating to heating systems are: poor maintenance, improper combustion or venting, exposure to flammable materials, and overheating

Here are some things you can do to reduce the risk of heating system fires:

Service your heating systems every year. Proper maintenance and calibration of fuel, combustion air, and venting are the key components of proper and safe operation. Improper combustion due to debris accumulation on the burners, or limited combustion air, increases the risk of carbon monoxide production. Failure of the heat exchanger, which is the primary barrier between the flame and the room air, also increases the risk of carbon monoxide production. Improper or failed venting to the exterior can also increase the risk of toxic gases entering the interior of the home. All of these factors can be assessed and reduced with annual inspection, service, and cleaning, performed by a qualified, licensed heating contractor.

Keep flammable materials away from heating systems. At least 12 inches of clearance should be maintained around furnaces, heat pumps, and baseboard heaters to reduce the risk of igniting flammable materials. This includes furniture, draperies, rugs or other household materials.

Protect your portable space heaters. These units should be kept at least 24 inches to 36 inches away from furniture, draperies, and other flammable materials. Space heaters should also be placed on level flooring and out of foot traffic pathways. They should never be left unattended or used around unsupervised children.

Maintain proper air flow through the forced air heating systems. Replacing air filters every three months and keeping furniture away from cold air returns will help maintain sufficient air flow throughout your heating system. This will allow it to operate efficiently and safely.

Water Heater Safety

Water heating appliances have very similar fire concerns as heating systems do. These concerns include exposure to flammable materials, improper combustion, and improper venting. However, besides the similar worries, water heaters also present other safety concerns worth noting.

In areas that are prone to earthquakes, water heaters should be strapped at the top and bottom, while also being fitted with flexible gas connectors. This will prevent movement and possible gas leaks in case of seismic movement.

When a water heater is installed in a garage or basement, the lower heating element should be elevated 18 inches off the ground. This will reduce the risk of igniting flammable gases that may come from gasoline tanks or paint cans. Newer Flammable Vapor Ignition Resistant (FVIR) water heaters are designed to prevent ignition of vapors and may be installed directly on to the floor.

Lastly, water heaters are easily capable of heating water to over 150°. Within seconds, water at this temperature can cause third degree burns to exposed skin. This is a significant safety hazard, especially for children and the elderly. The temperature setting for the water heater is controlled by the user and should be set to about 120°, which is much safer for direct skin contact.

Here are steps you can take to reduce the risk of water heater-related incidents:

Keep flammable materials away from the water heater. Do not store items on top or within 12 inches of your water heater. Be sure that water heaters are properly elevated if necessary.

Make sure earthquake strapping is secure. Water heaters should be securely strapped at the top and bottom of the unit, with thick straps that are screwed to the structural wall behind the unit. Earthquake strapping is available at most neighborhood hardware stores.

Lower the thermostat to prevent scald hazards. Adjust your water heater thermostat to the lowest setting that you are comfortable with to prevent scalding hazards.

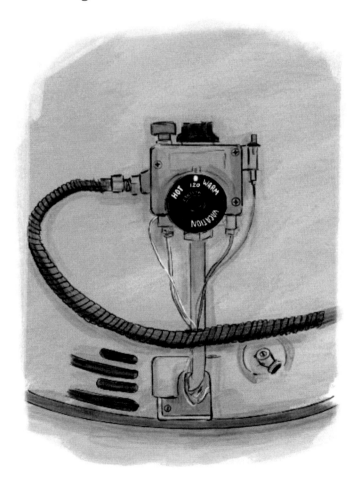

Natural Gas Safety

Natural gas is a reliable energy source for appliances, including heating systems, water heaters, cooktops, ovens, clothes dryers, fireplaces, and barbecues. It is also a great energy source for secondary systems, including pool/spa heaters and backup generators.

The natural gas supply to a home runs through underground piping that emerges at the home's gas meter. The main valve, just below the meter, controls the gas flow through the meter and to the home. Operating the main valve is only necessary if there is an emergency and/or if no local shut off is accessible or provided.

Additional gas shutoff valves should be installed at each gas appliance to allow for service of the appliance.

Natural gas does not naturally have a detectable odor or smell, so an ingredient called mercaptan is added to give gas the smell of rotten eggs. This smell is intended to get your attention quickly and elicit a reaction.

If you smell rotten eggs in your home, first check the burners on your cooking surface. It is not uncommon for a burner to be opened slightly if a knob is bumped. Additionally, gas ovens may release a little gas as they go through their ignition process. If you identify the smell and are sure it is coming from your stove top, close the open burner valve and open all windows to vent the gas out of the space.

If you cannot identify and eliminate the source of the gas, evacuate the home immediately, and call 911 for assistance.

In an emergency where you must shut off the main valve at the gas meter, it is important to keep a gas shut off wrench at the meter. Use the wrench to rotate the main valve ¼ turn, putting the valve perpendicular to the piping. This will cut off the gas supply to the home; however, residual gas and pressure will remain in the piping between the main valve and the appliances.

While homeowners should be able to shut off the gas supply to their own home if necessary, it is highly recommended that your utility company be called to restore the gas supply when it is safe. Not only do they provide the very important service of testing each connection for leakage, but they also can relight pilot lights where necessary.

Here are some things you can do to reduce the risk of gas fires:

Know where your gas meter is. Gas meters are typically along an exterior wall, in the front half of the home. Be sure the meter is always accessible and clear any vegetation growth to allow for easy access.

Place a gas shut off wrench at the main gas meter. As mentioned above, it is important to keep a gas shut off wrench at the meter in case of significant leakage or other emergencies. It is important you be able to shut off the valve immediately, if a situation does occur.

Know where the appliance shutoffs are located. Any natural gas appliance should have an accessible gas shut off valve. For free-standing appliances, it will likely be difficult to access, as it requires pulling the appliance out from the wall. However, with cooktops, the valve should be accessible in the cabinet below each unit.

Know what natural gas smells like. To understand the smell of natural gas and the mercaptan additive, smell a small bit of gas - just enough to become familiar with the scent. Before doing so, open the windows in your kitchen. Turn on the burner of your range or cooktop quickly, to bypass the spark ignition. A rotten egg odor, the smell of mercaptan, will be quickly detectable. Remember to shut off your range within seconds after smelling the gas. Stay aware of this smell and act quickly if you smell it again.

Clothes Dryer Safety

The NFPA reports that over 4,000 home fires per year are attributed to poorly maintained clothes dryers, primarily due to lint accumulation.[7]

Here is one key step you can take to reduce the risk of clothes dryer fires:

Clean the lint. Clean your lint filter on a regular basis and, on occasion, clean the space behind the lint filter. Additionally, replace the flexible ductwork running from the rear of the dryer to its exterior discharge each year. If you have rigid metal ductwork, this should also be cleaned periodically to get rid of any accumulated debris between the dryer and the exterior discharge. These steps will reduce the risk of dryer fires and improve the efficiency of the dryer itself.

Smoking Safety

The NFPA reports that fires caused by smoking materials were responsible for an average of 18,100 home structure fires each year between 2010 and 2014. These fires caused $476 million in property damage and 590 fire deaths annually.[8]

If you would like to stop smoking, the American Cancer Society (www.cancer.org) offers resources and information to help you quit.

If you must smoke, please follow these guidelines to reduce the risk of starting fires:

Don't smoke in bed or on upholstered furniture. Most smoking-related fire deaths are related to smoking materials igniting bedding or upholstery.

Smoke outside. Stay away from flammable materials and use deep, wide ashtrays on a secure, sturdy table. Always be sure that the ashes and butts are completely extinguished. You can do this by soaking them in water or covering them with sand. Do not throw your used butts into plants or onto the ground around the home.

Keep matches and lighters out of reach of children. I imagine that we all know someone who started a fire as a kid because they were playing with matches. As adults though, we recognize that children and matches just don't mix.

Vegetation Safety

There are a number of benefits to clearing excess vegetation around the exterior of your home. Among these is reducing your home's risk of fire.

Creating a separation from combustible brush and grasses from around your home reduces the risk of a wildfire spreading to the structure of your home. This defensible space is recommended to extend 30 feet or more around your home. Unfortunately, the occurrence of fast-moving wildfires in populated neighborhoods has become more common in recent years, especially in the western half of the US. Further information about wildfires and protecting your home can be found at www.readyforwildfire.org.

Clearing vegetation from the overhead electrical service lines to your house reduces the risk of electrical arcing and ignition of tree branches. It also reduces the risk of damage to the service wires as well as minimizes the chance of losing power in windy or icy conditions. You should have at least 3 feet of clearance around your electrical service wires, starting from where they attach to your house all the way up to the connection at the utility pole.

Here are some recommendations you can follow to prevent vegetation-related fires:

Clear vegetation from electrical service wires. When tree branches come in contact with the electrical supply wiring that is running between the utility pole and your electrical service mast, there is an increased risk of sparking. Either tree branches could catch fire or the items on the ground could ignite due to falling sparks. If tree branches are in contact with electrical service wiring, contact your utility provider to get the branches trimmed.

Clear any vegetation and debris from your roof. This includes branches and leaves that have accumulated in roof valleys or in the gutter system around the perimeter of your home. This will preserve the lifespan of your roofing materials, allow for proper control of roof runoff when raining, and reduce the risk of embers, from a nearby fireplace or wildfire, igniting dry debris on the roof.

Clear vegetation from around the fire hydrants. An obstructed or overgrown hydrant will slow fire service response times and may lead to firefighter injury, increased property damage, or delays in rescue responses. Do your local fire department a favor and keep hydrants in your neighborhood clear of vegetation growth or other obstacles.

CHAPTER 5 - PREPARE TO RESPOND TO FIRES

Despite efforts to prevent fires from starting in the first place, there is always a risk of a house fire starting, due to equipment failures, human error, or accidents. Having a plan to respond quickly if a fire does occur can certainly help protect your home and family.

Have Fire Extinguishers Available

Multi-purpose, dry chemical fire extinguishers are available at most home supply stores and are effective in extinguishing small fires, involving the three most common types of fuels in a home:

Class A fires occur in common combustible materials like wood, paper, and plastic.

Class B fires include flammable liquids and gases like paint, gasoline, and household cleaners.

Class C fires occur in electrical wiring, equipment, and appliances.

Here are some recommendations for using fire extinguishers in your home:

Place multi-purpose extinguishers in recommended areas. A multi-purpose extinguisher, with an ABC rating, should be placed in the kitchen, garage, and laundry room to eliminate small fires before they grow.

Check extinguisher gauges. If not in the green, replace the extinguisher.

Replace old fire extinguishers. Fire extinguishers have a lifespan of up to 10 years. To check the date of manufacture for your extinguishers, go to the manufacturer's website to translate the code stamped on the unit.

Practice using an extinguisher. When using a fire extinguisher, it is helpful to remember **PASS**, the acronym for **P**ull, **A**im, **S**queeze, and **S**weep.

Pull the pin out of the fire extinguisher handle.

Aim at the base of the fire, staying at least six to eight feet away.

Squeeze the handle to start the extinguishing agent.

Sweep side to side.

Install Smoke Alarms

A 2019 National Fire Protection Association (NFPA) report found that nearly 60% of fire fatalities occur in homes without working smoke alarms.[9]

The four factors that greatly affect the efficiency of smoke alarms include: their placement in proper locations, the age of the smoke alarm, the type of detection method used, and the reliability of the power supply.

Proper Placement

Smoke alarms are required to be placed in each bedroom, in the hallway outside bedrooms, and on each floor of the home, including basements and garages. Bedroom alarms should be installed on the ceiling near the interior door and no closer than 4 inches from a wall. Smoke alarms should be installed at least 10 feet away from kitchens, to avoid nuisance alarms when cooking.

Lifespan

Smoke alarms have a typical lifespan of up to ten years. With age, their ability to properly detect smoke and fire is greatly reduced. To determine the age of the smoke alarms installed in your home, check the label on the unit for a date of manufacture. If no date is listed, it is likely already older than ten years and should be replaced.

Detection Methods

In the early stages of a fire, smaller particles of soot, ash, and other toxic gases are released into the air. Smoke alarms sense these smaller particles using one of two detection methods.

Ionization alarms detect active flaming fires and are marked with a lowercase "i" in a circle.

Photoelectric alarms sense the smaller particles of a smoldering smoke fire and are marked with a lowercase "p" in a square or rectangle.

Dual sensor alarms utilize both ionization and photoelectric methods to detect flaming and smoldering fires, providing a broader response to household fires. These alarms are labeled with both the ionization and photoelectric markings. These units are recommended when installing new or replacement smoke alarms in the home.

Power Supply

In the past, we have recommended that smoke alarm batteries be changed twice a year. Recently, manufacturers have begun installing 10-year batteries in their smoke alarms to increase their reliability. As the rated life span of a smoke alarm is also ten years, these new batteries are essentially intended to last the lifetime of the unit.

Although a longer battery life makes a smoke alarm more reliable, we now run the risk of forgetting about them. In the past, when we would have to change the batteries in our smoke alarms twice a year, it was a helpful reminder of where each smoke alarm was and what the alarm sounds like. Now, with 10-year batteries, smoke alarms can be out of sight, out of mind. Consequently, the opportunity to expose our kids to smoke alarms can easily be lost. So, whether your smoke alarms have replaceable batteries or a lifetime 10-year battery, they should still be *tested* twice a year. A helpful timeline to go off of, which I used with my own family, is when you change your clocks for daylight savings time.

Here are some recommendations for using smoke alarms properly:

Install smoke alarms in proper locations. This includes in every bedroom and in the hallway on each floor of your home. The presence of working smoke alarms in these locations has greatly reduced the number of fire related deaths.

Check the age of smoke alarms. Replace older alarms with new, dual sensor alarms to provide the best protection from smoldering and flaming fires.

Change batteries and test smoke alarms twice a year. If using older alarms, change the 9-volt or AA batteries twice a year, but regardless of the battery life, all smoke alarms should be tested twice a year.

Install Carbon Monoxide Alarms

Carbon monoxide (CO) is a colorless and odorless gas that is the by-product of faulty fuel combustion and improper venting of exhaust. CO can displace the oxygen in your bloodstream, resulting in headache, weakness, dizziness, blurred vision, confusion, loss of consciousness, and possible death. CO poisoning kills hundreds of people each year.

CO alarms should also be installed in the hallways outside of sleeping areas and on each floor of your home. As CO dissipates relatively evenly, wall-mounted or ceiling-mounted units are equally effective.

Much like smoke alarms, CO alarms have a typical lifespan of approximately ten years. If you have a CO alarm that is older than that, it should be replaced as soon as possible, for maximum safety. CO alarm batteries should be changed and the units should be tested twice a year, along with smoke alarms.

Here are some recommendations for detecting carbon monoxide risks in your home:

Install carbon monoxide alarms in proper locations. This includes in the hallways outside of bedrooms and on each floor of your home.

Check the age of CO alarms. Replace CO alarms if older than ten years.

Change batteries and test CO alarms twice a year. If using older alarms, change the 9-volt or AA batteries twice a year. Even if you are using a newer model, regardless of the battery life, all CO alarms should be tested twice a year.

Prepare Bedside

Keeping some items under or beside each bed can improve the chances of everyone getting outside safely, in the case of an emergency that happens in the middle of the night.

Keep a flashlight and a whistle beside each bed. A strong flashlight can light up dark, smoke-filled spaces to help someone find their way to an exit and avoid any obstacles or other hazards. Additionally, it can help others locate someone who is stuck or not able to get out. A strong whistle can also help firefighters find someone who is trapped, while also being able to alert neighbors to the fire and the need for help.

Close your Door when Sleeping

Underwriters Labs conducted a study to show how quickly smoke and heat can enter through open bedroom doors.[10] In their simulation, they placed sensors and cameras around the interior of a two-bedroom model home. They left one-bedroom door open and the other closed, before beginning the test. A fire was then started in the living room, using a candle. The candle was placed in the corner of the couch and the resulting fire was allowed to grow. The study revealed that the air quality in the bedroom with the open door became deadly within 3 minutes of the fire starting. Quickly, there became insufficient oxygen, toxic levels of carbon monoxide, and temperatures exceeding 1000 degrees.

On the other hand, the environment in the bedroom with the closed door stayed survivable well beyond the start of the fire. There remained sufficient oxygen, elevated but survivable levels of carbon monoxide, and a temperature below 100 degrees. This difference in environments can have a significant impact on surviving a fire at night.

A video sharing further details can be found at www.closeyourdoor.org.

Clear Secondary Exits

When you think of an exit leading out of a bedroom, the interior door is most likely what comes to mind first. From a practical viewpoint, that pathway is always available, but in the case of a fire, smoke and heat may block the interior path between your bedroom door and an exterior exit.

Knowing this, it is important to identify another way out. A bedroom window should allow for an able-bodied person to climb out in an emergency or for a firefighter with an air pack to climb in. This requires the window to open at least 20 inches by 24 inches wide and that the bottom sill of the window be no more than 44 inches above the floor.

Here are some recommendations for preparing secondary exits:

Make sure all bedroom windows open easily. If any blinds or window treatments are installed, be sure they can be easily raised or pushed to the side to clear the access to the window. Also, be sure the window screen is easily removable. If it can't be removed easily, have the screen repaired or replaced as necessary.

Clear obstacles outside windows. Be sure there are no obstacles outside each window, including overgrown vegetation, additional structures, or debris that block the way out.

Install fire ladders. If there is a drop greater than six feet, consider using a fire escape ladder and be sure that everyone knows how to use it.

Clear the route from each window to the meeting place. Check the route from each window to the front yard. Be sure there is no fencing, vegetation, locked gates, or structures that prevent getting to the front yard easily.

CHAPTER 6 - PRACTICE YOUR FIRE PLAN

While knowledge of all the information we have covered earlier in this book is important in preventing and responding to smaller fires, the most important step in surviving a house fire is committing the time to plan for a safe evacuation. This year, make Father's Day extra special by making it the day that you and your family create and practice your own family fire plan.

Begin by setting aside some time, gather everyone together, and talk about the goal of getting everyone out safely, in the event of a fire.

Reinforce that this is not about creating fear, but, instead, meant to do quite the opposite. As a family, preparing and discussing what to do during a fire may actually reduce fear when it comes to a real-life emergency. Most importantly, include everyone in the family when discussing and practicing the steps to prevent fires and getting out safely, if one does occur.

Be prepared to answer questions that may come up and take these questions seriously. If a tough question gets asked, one that you are unsure of the answer to, research the answer together and talk about what you find. These discussions are one of the most important parts in establishing a plan. Everyone needs to feel that they have an equal part in it.

Here are topics that are important to discuss:

Sources of fires in your home. Talk about the places in your home where fires commonly begin, including the kitchen, laundry room, and garage, and discuss the recommendations made earlier in this book to reduce the risk of fires from starting in these areas.

Preventing fires in your home. There are many things we can all do and work towards together, to reduce the risk of fires and reduce the risk of a small fire escalating. As a family, talk about the ways you can control and extinguish fires in any of these areas, including using fire extinguishers.

Fire behavior in your home. Talk about what fire needs to burn and how it's likely to spread within your home. Go over where fires may occur and which interior hallways or doorways may be blocked by smoke, flames, and heat as the fire continues to grow.

Sound the alarms. Test the smoke and carbon monoxide alarms around the house and listen to how they sound. When everyone can recognize the sound of the alarms, see how they sound from behind a closed bedroom door or from a different part of the house. See if everyone can identify where the alarm is by how it sounds in each room.

Stay low. Talk about how smoke and heat rise and how staying low on the ground will make it easier to breathe while finding a way out. To simulate a dark or smoke-filled room, crawl on the floor and find the bedroom door with your eyes closed.

Check doors for heat. Talk about how closed doors get hot when there is fire on the other side. Practice feeling every door for heat before opening it. Run the back of your hand from the bottom of the door up, and then feel the doorknob for heat. If the door appears cool enough, open the door slowly and look out for fire and smoke.

Alert everyone. Emphasize the importance of alerting the rest of the family if anyone were to find a fire. Practice yelling out to the rest of the household and alert everyone on what you are doing and/or what they should do as well. Talk about how if everyone is asleep, you should grab a whistle and blow it to wake others in the home and alert them that you are getting out.

Help others out. As a family, talk about how everyone can help each other get out, including small children, people with disabilities, and the elderly, too.

Find secondary exits. If you are unable to use the bedroom door, you will need to be able use the bedroom window to evacuate. Identify other landmarks within the room, such as heat registers, windows, or closets to help easily locate your safety window. It can be helpful to place a night light in an outlet directly below the window to provide a beacon. Be sure that everyone can reach the window sill. This may require moving a small piece of furniture to step up onto.

Climb out the window. Be sure that everyone is able to open the windows fully and that the window screens can easily be removed. Screens are typically removable by pulling tabs on one side and pushing them outward. Once everyone is able to reach the window sill, double check that there are no obstacles blocking the ground directly outside the window. Any landscaping or structures should be cleared to allow for easy exit. If you are on a second story level or more than six feet above the ground, a fire escape ladder should be available and practiced at this time.

What if you can't get out? In some scenarios, you may not be able to get out. If you are stuck in a room, keep the door closed and tightly pack clothing at the base of the door to prevent smoke and heat from coming under. After you are sure that the gap is secure, open the window and call for help. This can be done by yelling, blowing your bedside whistle, shining a flashlight, or doing anything to let someone know that you are there and in need of immediate help.

Set your meeting place. Consider a landmark in the front yard that everyone is familiar with, such as the mailbox, a light pole, a noticeable tree, or nearby fence post. Discuss how to get help from neighbors and how to alert them if their homes are at risk.

Get to the meeting place. Identify the pathway from each bedroom window to a meeting place in the front yard. This pathway should avoid any obstacles, such as fences, hard to open gates, overgrown landscaping, sheds, or other barriers that will make it harder to get to safety.

Ask the hard questions. Talk about what to do if everyone has not gotten out, including family members or pets. Once safely out, you should never go back inside the home, but there may still be ways to help someone from outside their window. If someone is still stuck inside, tell the arriving fire crews, and they will begin rescue operations immediately. However, if everyone is confirmed to be out, they will be able to focus on fire control.

FIREFIGHTING AND FIRE SAFETY

In this section, we will discuss how emergency services respond to a fire and what we can do to improve fire safety, moving forward.

CHAPTER 7 - FIREFIGHTING STRATEGIES

The amazing thing about emergency services is no matter what problem you are having, there is always someone available to help. That was one of the things that attracted me most to volunteering for the fire service.

What Happens When You Call 911?

Your call will be directed to an emergency dispatch center somewhere in your local area. Dispatch centers are staffed 24/7 and have specialists trained to ask you the right questions – to get the information fast. Once they know your situation, they will be able to assign the best resources and immediately send them to the right location.

You may expect being assigned the best resource to be easy (as in a fire engine will go to a structure fire and a police officer to a bank robbery), but emergency responses are more complex than they seem. Any given emergency may require a variety of resources.

For example, a bad traffic accident may require: law enforcement for traffic control and documentation, including witness statements and photographs of the accident scene; fire department for stabilizing vehicles, controlling any fire hazards or fuel spills, extracting patients from damaged vehicles, and emergency medical assessment; ambulance service for transporting people to an emergency room; utility services if power lines or other service lines are affected; animal control if there are any animals involved; and tow trucks to clear the damaged vehicles.

Communication between all of these resources is coordinated directly through the 911 dispatch center. The more complex an incident is, the more resources are requested and the more complications need to be anticipated.

When a 911 call comes in, dispatchers try to gain as much information about the scene as possible. This helps them prepare the responders for what they will face when they arrive. This may include information on specific addresses and cross streets, how many people are involved in the incident, if anyone is hurt or missing, or if there are any other dangers present, including weapons, animals, or chemical spills. Because fire crews must begin to define their strategy well before they even arrive on the scene, dispatchers provide crucial information to the responding fire crews.

Next, dispatchers try to provide guidance to callers on how they can help the situation, while emergency responders are in route. This may include guiding the caller to get to a safe location, eliminate any hazards, or provide bystander medical care.

Fire department protocols dictate the proper number and types of resources to be dispatched, depending on the type of the emergency. For example, confirmed structure fires may require two engines, a ladder truck, two medic units, a battalion chief, and one or more support trucks. This alert has likely been sent out within 60 seconds of the call starting.

Fire departments typically have goals for their response time, which is the time between the moment the alert is sent out to the fire crew rolling out the door. Ideally, this response time is between one to three minutes, depending on the size of the department.

While on route, the dispatcher will provide the responding crews with even more information about the structure and the extent of the fire based on the caller's information.

The response time from the fire station to the fire scene is dependent on both the distance and the availability of a direct route. For most larger cities, this may be within five minutes, but for more rural areas and smaller towns, the response time may be longer.

The first engine that arrives on scene has the responsibility of providing an initial assessment of the fire, reporting to incoming resources, and establishing the first fire attack lines. They may also be responsible for establishing the water supply from the closest hydrant. After arriving on the scene, these tasks may take up to three minutes.

It is important to note that the time between a caller dialing 911 and having fire crews spray water on the fire may be ten minutes or more. In the earlier chapter on fire behavior, we discussed how the time until flashover occurs has decreased drastically. Even with the best possible response time from the fire department, a home may still become fully involved and deadly well before the first crews are able to begin putting the fire out.

Firefighter Equipment

In the fire service, there is a simple goal to, "put the wet stuff on the red stuff." This means, extinguishing fires by applying water to burning materials is a primary function of the response.

Fire engines may arrive on the scene with a short-term supply of 500 to 1,000 gallons of water on board, but connection to a constant water supply, such as a hydrant, is still essential.

Most municipal water systems provide hydrant systems around the area they serve. These distribution systems are designed to provide a reliable source of water at any time.

All hydrants have multiple outlets called ports. The larger opening is called the steamer port and connects to the supply hose from a fire engine. The smaller ports can also be connected to a second engine, allowing multiple water supplies.

STEAMER
PORT

SIDE
PORT

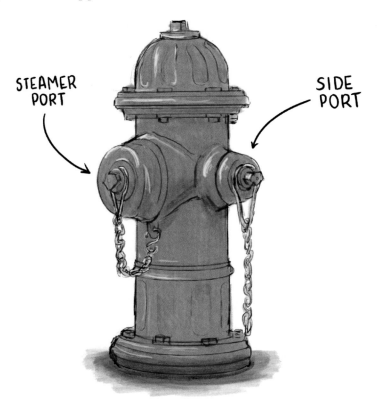

Steamer ports have been developed with differing sizes, from 3 inches to 5 inches in diameter. While local fire departments commonly configure their engines to connect to their own hydrants, problems can arise if they travel outside their area to assist other fire departments. This emerged as a significant issue during the 1991 Oakland Hills Fire, as engines from neighboring cities were not able to connect to local hydrants due to differing sizes of port connections.

As the need for a universal connector emerged, the Storz-type coupling was established as a standard that provides a rapid connection. While some hydrants are fitted with Storz-type couplings, most engines are equipped with adapters to connect any size threaded connection to a Storz connector. Primary supply hoses are commonly fitted with Storz connectors on both ends.

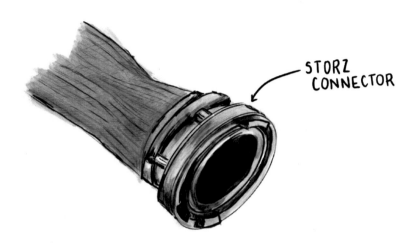

STORZ CONNECTOR

Supply hoses run from a hydrant to the engine. These are typically 3 inches to 5 inches in diameter and are designed to transport large amounts of water, a short distance to the engine. Most engines will have up to 1,000 feet of supply hose on board. Engines that pump will then take that water supply and provide a number of individual hoses, called attack lines, with sole control of water pressure on each line.

Attack lines come in two common sizes, 1¾ inches and 2½ inches. These lines are easier to navigate through a home and can be managed by one or two firefighters. Individual 50-foot lengths of hose can be joined together by couplings to extend 500 feet or more. The nozzles on the ends of these hoses are adjustable to provide the firefighter with full control of the stream width and spread.

FIRE HOSE COUPLINGS

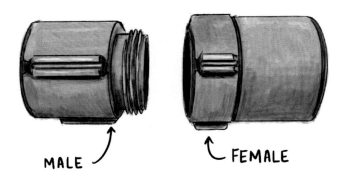

MALE   FEMALE

The path of the water from the hydrant to the fire has a number of points of control but must be constant and reliable, to ensure safe and efficient extinguishment.

Firefighters have a number of tools to help fight fire, move obstacles, and protect themselves. A number of these tools and methods have been in use for decades due to their simplicity and evolution with firefighter input. Even so, other tools emerge today, as we make advances in technology.

Firefighters have a variety of ladders and ropes that allow them to access points that are higher or lower than ground level. This includes upper floors of multi-story buildings and roofs.

There are a number of hand tools that give firefighters the ability to open, cut, puncture, and pull. These motions can allow a firefighter to create new openings and clear obstacles that prevent movement or access. This may involve opening a locked door, breaking a window, pulling down a ceiling, or cutting a hole. These tools must be extremely durable and even more reliable because the life of a resident and/or a firefighter may depend on them.

The firefighter's personal protective equipment (PPE) is the most important tool that he or she uses. PPE includes a fire-resistant duty uniform, steel toe duty boots, turnouts (the fire, liquid, and heat resistant pants and coat), fire boots, fire resistant gloves, an air pack, a mask, a hood, and a helmet. Each of these items protects the firefighter from heat, smoke, and cuts or abrasions; however, when all of these objects are properly worn, the firefighter can have an imposing, if not frightening, silhouette. For younger children, the shape of the equipment and the sound of a firefighter "on air" (breathing through the air mask) can be frightening and dissuade them from wanting to be found.

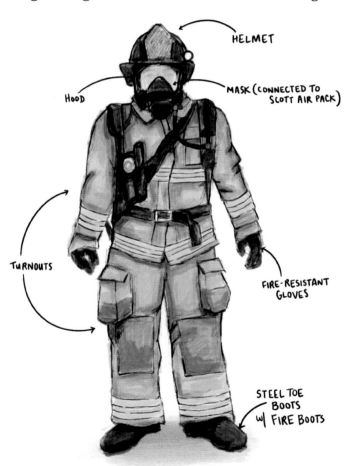

HELMET

HOOD

MASK (CONNECTED TO SCOTT AIR PACK)

TURNOUTS

FIRE-RESISTANT GLOVES

STEEL TOE BOOTS w/ FIRE BOOTS

To expose children to a firefighter in full PPE, I strongly recommend taking advantage of community events where the fire department is present. Ask the local fire fighters to show your child what the equipment looks like off, what it does, and what it looks like when it is worn. This can reduce the fear and uncertainty in an emergency situation.

Newer technology has improved a firefighter's ability to assess risks and locate victims. Infrared technology, which sees heat differences, has given firefighters new vision when trying to locate hidden areas of fire. This helps them reduce the risk of re-ignition, while also locating victims concealed from view, whether unconscious or hiding.

Secondly, visual displays within firefighter masks are showing promise as a method for providing critical information to firefighters. This information can include details on the activities of those around them and the status of their own equipment.

The use of airborne drones also gives incident commanders a higher viewpoint to assess fire scenes and the surrounding areas for hazards and fire growth.

Methods and Strategies

In simple terms, the strategy for fighting a structural fire is based on a number of goals, the most important goal being the safety of the occupants and the firefighters themselves.

While en route to the fire, the dispatcher conveys information from the caller to the fire fighters. This may include sharing the type of structure they are heading towards and whether it is known if anyone is still inside.

With knowledge of the neighborhood and the use of maps, the crew determines the location of the closest hydrant and where to place the engine. They want to be in the best position to attack the fire, while also minimizing the risk to the crew or the apparatus.

Upon arrival at the scene, the crew of the first-in engine has a number of extremely important roles.

The officer starts a "scene size-up", which is a quick assessment describing the type of structure and the extent of fire or smoke visible from the front. This starts to paint a picture for the other incoming units. The officer performs a walk around the perimeter of the structure to assess the further specifics of the structure, as well as to see if there are any hazards that were not noticed from the front. They will also be able to learn more about the extent of the fire.

Each side of the home has a designated label, allowing the crew to communicate clearly. The side of the home that faces the engine placement, which is often the street side of the home, is the Alpha side. Then moving clockwise around the building, the left side is called the Bravo side, the rear of the home is the Charlie side, and the right side is the Delta side.

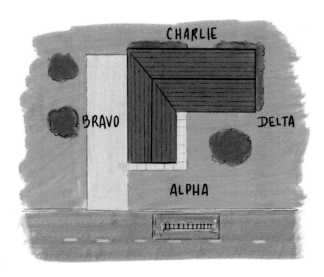

This creates common identifiers for all of the crews and gives specific information regarding the location of the fire and where it may be spreading. This language will help them determine the strategy for fighting the fire.

An awareness of common floor plans in the neighborhood helps predict where residents may be located. For many homes, the living spaces are downstairs while the bedrooms are upstairs. With heavy smoke and flames coming from upstairs windows, there is an indication that the fire is in a bedroom.

During the time the officer is assessing the scene, the other firefighters prepare for attacking the fire by establishing a water supply and pulling the first attack line. Checking with the occupants or neighbors, they will also determine if any individuals remain in the home. This is the time where a very important decision is made. If there are still occupants in the home, the officer will make the decision to send a team into the structure before other crews have arrived.

Once the officer has completed their walk around, they will broadcast their scene size-up, providing information of what they have seen, what they have done, what they are doing, and what they need the next crew to accomplish. This may sound like:

"Engine 79 is on scene of a wood framed, single family home. Flames and heavy smoke are visible from the second floor Alpha side. We have pulled an attack line and will be entering the front door for rescue. Next-in engine should establish a water supply and pull a secondary attack line."

There is a common saying, "risk a lot to save a lot; risk little to save a little." This means a greater risk will be taken to save a life, but when no lives are at risk, less risk is pursued. An empty building will be fought from the outside until it is safe to enter, but the risk to enter a building without backup crews ready may be undertaken to rescue an occupant.

With occupants still in the home, a rescue involves the primary crew going in with a hose line, if necessary, with the sole purpose of rescue. In case additional support is necessary, the engineer stays outside and keeps in radio contact with the crew. It is a high-risk operation for a crew to enter a burning home without a backup crew on scene. Risk a lot to save a lot.

When the home is vacant but there is still much inside that can be saved, an offensive attack will begin. This involves the crew going inside with attack hoses to attack the seat of the fire. However, this happens only if additional crews are on scene for backup. Risk little to save a little.

When the home is confirmed vacant and there is little chance of saving it, the fire attack will become purely defensive and focus on preventing the fire from spreading to neighboring homes.

For most fires, a battalion chief takes over leadership control at the fire scene, dictating the assignment for each crew and being accountable for their location.

Heat and Smoke Ventilation

The goal of the fire attack is to eliminate the fire and the heat accumulated within a structure. This includes cooling the material with water and cooling the air by venting.

There are two methods of venting to remove heated air and gases. Some departments may place a crew on the roof to cut openings, allowing heat and smoke to escape, utilizing natural convection to replace hot air with cooler outside air.

The other method involves opening windows and placing a positive pressure ventilation (PPV) fan at the front entrance, to push the heat and gases out. Both methods are effective, but the risks and damages can vary.

As the fire starts to be controlled, crews will work to protect belongings within the home, not only from fire but from smoke and water damage, as well.

Once the majority of the fire is controlled, crews will then work to locate and extinguish smaller areas of burning materials, including opening walls and ceilings and removing burning materials.

Firefighter Safety

Over the last thirty years in the fire service, the focus on firefighter safety has changed significantly. By its nature, firefighting is a dangerous profession, with almost daily exposure to extreme heat, toxic gases and chemicals, infectious diseases, and a seemingly endless list of other types of hazards. Systemic improvements in training, equipment, and written procedures has resulted in a remarkable decrease in firefighter injuries and deaths. But, the types of hazards that firefighters are asked to respond to continues to grow, including types of chemical spills, radioactive leakage, and terrorist attacks.

CHAPTER 8 - BUILDING CODES & FIRE SAFETY

E arlier, we touched on some changes to building codes that have improved survival in structure fires; however, there is more to be done in standardizing fire safety codes around the country.

First, let's understand the process of developing and adopting building codes, specifically those that relate to fire safety. Professional organizations, such as the National Fire Protection Association (NFPA), are made up of engineers and fire service professionals. These professionals are responsible for assessing fire safety concerns and making recommendations in the form of the fire safety codes. These codes are regularly reviewed, amended, and published every few years.

The goals of these code recommendations are to: prevent fire hazards, improve the systems of alerting residents to fire activity, slow the spread of a fire within a structure, improve the survivability and egress pathways for residents, reduce property damage and spread to neighboring structures, and improve the safety of fire service personnel.

Often, code recommendations are initiated in response to emerging fire safety concerns, increases in fire deaths, injuries, and/or property damage, or awareness of poor design and/or installation methods.

Once new fire codes are published, local and state governmental jurisdictions have the option to consider adopting part, or all, of the new recommended codes. Feedback from local businesses, industry organizations, trade unions, and the general public are considered. This can spark political debate among groups and include concerns for expenses and time, which are necessary in implementing changes in the construction process and receiving a critical review of the predictive data. Often, pushback from industry groups can significantly slow, or even derail, attempts to adopt specific recommendations.

The process from initial consideration to eventual adoption by a government entity can take many years. While new recommendations may be in response to an increase in injuries and damages or the realization of faulty design or installation methods, they also should be forward thinking. This can help account for changes in construction trends, lifestyle changes, energy efficiency demands, and environmental impacts.

Some of the natural barriers to acceptance of new building codes include: increased cost of construction, lack of consumer knowledge and demand, environmental considerations, and lack of technological efficiency.

With an increase in consumer education on the life safety aspects and development of improved technology to reduce costs, these obstacles may eventually be overcome.

An example of the slow process of adoption is the effort to install residential solar power systems. For decades, personal solar power was not cost effective and was considered a bit of a punchline. However, with recent improvements in technological efficiency and reduction of net cost, residential solar power is now becoming quite common.

Campaigns to educate the public are slow to show impact and by our own nature, people may fail to personally identify with stories of fire emergencies and deaths. We are more prone to feel such situations will not happen to us, due to differences in our homes, our lifestyles, or our standard of living. What can be difficult to remember is that fire behavior is inherently ignorant to many of those factors. Nowhere in the fire triangle is the consideration for brand name or retail cost. And whatever your political or religious beliefs, all of us are susceptible to the same forces of physics. When things get hot, they burn – no matter what.

Secondly, the prevalence of injuries and deaths due to fires is far less common than deaths from other factors (i.e.: heart disease, cancer, suicide, car accidents, etc.). However, if my child was to die in a fire, fire safety would become the most important thing to me and my family.

79

So, let's discuss the state of a few building code adoptions that are still in process around the country and what may be responsible for their slow adoption.

Smoke and Carbon Monoxide Alarms

Over the years, many of my home inspection clients have asked where smoke alarms are required to be installed. There can be a lot of confusion about this since local building codes may differ, so it is best to check with your local building officials for specific code requirements in your area.

In all 50 states, though, smoke alarms are required to be installed in sleeping areas and in hallways, on each floor. This has been a significant step in improving home safety. Since the adoption of these requirements and the widespread presence of smoke alarms, the number of fire related deaths has been greatly reduced.

However, while technological improvements in alarms have been made, they have not been incorporated into these requirements. Carbon Monoxide (CO) alarms are required in only 47 states, leaving Oklahoma, Texas, and Hawaii without such requirements. The development of combination smoke/CO alarms eliminates the need for multiple devices and should allow for requiring CO alarms in all 50 states in the future.

As we discussed earlier in this book, combination smoke alarms are now able to detect two types of common fires, both flaming and smoldering fires, but only three states have added dual sensor alarms as a requirement in new construction.

The cost of smoke alarms is relatively small, compared to other fire safety features. However, cost fails to be a sufficient argument against adopting universal requirements for combination smoke/CO alarms that feature dual sensors in all residential homes.

Fire Sprinklers

Requiring fire sprinklers in newly-constructed, single family homes was introduced into the building codes in 2006 and has been part of the codes ever since. In that time, only California and Maryland have adopted the code requiring fire sprinklers in new constructions. Nineteen other states allow their local jurisdictions to adopt these codes on their own, but still do not mandate it statewide.

NFPA data shows deaths in homes with fire sprinklers are reduced by 80%, alongside a 70% reduction in property damage.[11] These numbers represent real lives and property that have been saved.

Resistance to the adoption of fire sprinkler requirements has been significant. In fact, 29 states have actually banned their local jurisdictions from adopting fire sprinkler codes.

Opponents cite the cost of installation outweighs the number of lives saved. This is an economic decision that makes assumptions about home buyers and cannot be substantiated. According to NFPA calculations, the average cost of installing fire sprinklers is about $1.35 per square foot.[12] For the typical 1500 square foot house, that adds just over $2,000 to the cost of construction.

Garage Fire Barriers

Most consumers are unaware of the requirements for fire barriers between the garage and living spaces that slow the rapid spread of fire from the garage to the rest of the home. The requirements for an effective barrier include a solid core door with self-closing hinges between the garage and the living space. Penetrations in this door, such as for pet doors, violate this requirement.

Additionally, no openings or penetrations in the wall between the garage space and the interior living spaces should be visible. No openings into the attic space or crawl space should be present either.

Failure of the garage fire barrier was a common defect reported in many of my home inspections. Enforcement of these requirements for continuous fire barriers should be improved through consumer education and possible insurance incentives.

AFCI Circuits

Arc fault circuit interrupters (AFCI) are devices that sense an electrical circuit that is arcing, creating a rapid flow of electricity, which will then overheat quickly. This arcing may develop due to damage to the electrical wiring. Damage can occur from animals or inadvertent contact with a metal nail or other component. AFCI devices can sense this condition and shut itself off before damage can occur.

Requiring AFCI breakers on electrical circuits can do a great deal in reducing the risk of electrical fires. Each individual AFCI breaker may cost between $30 to $50, depending on the number of circuits within a home. The use of AFCIs is a recent addition to the National Electrical Code but has yet to attain universal acceptance.

Future Codes

Due to new residential styles that are emerging, such as tiny houses and short-term vacation rentals, there will be a need for further evaluation of fire safety issues and resulting code recommendations.

Community service groups, such as the Consumer Product Safety Commission (CPSC), the American Red Cross, and the National Fire Protection Association (NFPA), as well as government entities, such as the Federal Emergency Management Association (FEMA) and state fire marshal offices, should continue to do the important work of educating consumers on fire safety. They should also help implement improvements, which may increase consumer knowledge and demand for further safety changes.

It is important to consider that building codes should continue to focus on how we use residential structures while also incorporating how people instinctively respond in emergency situations. Architects and engineers can choose to design spaces and systems that dictate how people should act, but the reality is people will respond in a way that is natural and based on their own fears and experiences.

Building codes should be based on realistic human behavior, rather than engineering ideals. With this in mind, codes should begin to address improving options for rapid egress, including easier removal of window screens and window treatments, fire ladders for multi-story buildings, and easier access to climb out of bathroom windows.

Costs vs. Incentives

Arguments against improving fire safety codes will continue to be made, regarding the cost of implementing safety changes and who should be responsible for paying for them. But perhaps it is time to incorporate what we know about what has worked in the past in different industries.

The adoption of residential solar power, energy efficient appliances, and electric and hybrid vehicles have all been expedited by federal and state tax breaks, credits, and other financial incentives.

Additionally, insurance companies who provide discounts for using car alarms to prevent property losses have recently begun to incentivize the use of safe driving tracking devices to encourage safe driving behaviors.

Both government and industry can already influence adoption of systems through setting rules and establishing incentives. They should now direct those tools into making fire safety a priority.

As consumers, we also have a role to play in making fire safety a priority.

Let's implement tax incentives for homeowners to encourage investment in fire safety, such as installing fire sprinklers in new and existing homes, improving alarm systems to prevent smoke and carbon monoxide deaths, replacing unsafe and inefficient heating systems that are susceptible to initiating fires, improving standards for emergency egress (particularly in multi-story buildings), and improving 911 systems to cooperate better with cell phone technology.

Let's reduce the number of fire victims dying in homes where fire spreads rapidly without an effective fire suppression system and without any effective alarm.

Let's reduce the number of firefighters who are injured or killed as they try to control fires that quickly get out of control because they had no active fire suppression system or were forced to attempt rescue in a home where someone was not able to get out on their own.

Let's encourage insurance companies to provide discounts to property owners who make improvements in fire safety to reduce possible property damage, as they do for our vehicles, or for undergoing training in reducing the risk of fires starting, using fire extinguishers and establishing fire escape plans.

Let's show some real support for community service organizations, such as the American Red Cross, who provide training in fire prevention and CPR, while also responding to disasters with immediate support and continued services that serve fire victims, well beyond the fire.

The burden of being fire safe and protecting our own families, neighbors, and community falls on each of us.

CHAPTER 9 - PREPARING FOR OTHER DISASTERS

Shortly after my wife and I moved to North Carolina in 1992, a tornado watch was announced on the radio. This was very new to us.

We both grew up in the San Francisco Bay Area, so we knew about earthquakes. We rode out the Loma Prieta earthquake in 1989 and countless other smaller earthquakes. We never got warnings that earthquakes were coming, they just happened.

But a tornado watch means that conditions are prime for tornado development.

We grabbed our wedding photo album, pulled a mattress over the top of us in the bathtub, and braced for the worst.

Then the phone rang. Who would possibly be calling when conditions outside were so dangerous? It kept ringing because we didn't have an answering machine.

I felt that if the call was from our family on the west coast, I wanted to let them know we were safe and assure them that we were going to be okay. So, I headed out from the protected bathtub, leaving my wife and wedding photos behind.

Turns out, it was our friends from just down the street. They were heading out to dinner and wanted to know if we wanted to meet up. I breathlessly replied, "But, there is a tornado watch!"

Silence on the other end and then suddenly, unsympathetic laughter.

Apparently, tornado watches occurred constantly in North Carolina during spring and were something we actually learned to take very casually, over time.

Decades later, however, the teasing still continues.

We did not see any significant tornado or hurricane activity during the years we lived in North Carolina, nor during the few years we were in Houston. We were lucky.

But no matter where you live, there are wind storms, ice storms, traffic jams, train derailments, and all sorts of bad things happening around the world that disrupt people's lives. These events impede travel, interrupt our communications, and/or make us lose power.

Take a moment to recognize what risks you and your family face in your area and consider how you can store supplies and establish energy sources. This will help to keep your family safe, warm, and fed during any type of disaster.

Consider what items you need to bring with you in case of evacuation and plan how you can communicate with others around and outside of the area.

Know your neighbors, check on them, and see what they need to stay safe.

Get yourself involved in groups and organizations that help in a disaster. Many fire departments offer training in Community Emergency Response Teams (CERT). Work with your church or school to establish caches of disaster supplies and establish disaster plans. Contribute your time by volunteering with the American Red Cross.

Assemble disaster kits for your home, car, and workplace. Things that are generally recommended include:

1. Three-day supply of drinkable water and food
2. Prescription medicines
3. First aid kit
4. Extra diapers
5. Flashlights and batteries
6. A wireless radio
7. Blankets, pillows or other sentimental personal items
8. Extra cash
9. Food, water and any comfort items for any pets

There are a number of lists with recommended items to keep in an emergency kit. These lists are available on websites like the *American Red Cross* (www.redcross.org) and the *Federal Emergency Management Administration* (www.fema.gov).

CONCLUSION

Just like you, I struggle with balancing the demands of my career, family, and everything else in the world. But I am a dad who loves his family and wants to protect them in any way I can.

The recommendations in this book come from my professional training and personal experience. During home inspections, I would give my clients a checklist of safety recommendations and explain the reasons why smoke and carbon monoxide alarms should be installed near bedrooms and that they should test them twice a year. I would also tell them why maintaining their furnaces was important, why fireplaces should be cleaned and inspected by a chimney sweep, and why windows should be accessible for emergency exit.

But even in doing this, I was still missing how important it was to bring these recommendations together and develop a plan to reduce the risk of fires in my own home.

The fire service gave me opportunities to provide similar information about smoke alarms and fire extinguishers to the public, but I also had the chance to show children the protective gear we wear and the tools we use.

As a parent, I wanted to share my experience and knowledge with my family. With numerous resources out there, advising and explaining pieces of this puzzle, my goal on Father's Day was to bring everything together and create a strong fire safety plan for me and my family.

We didn't have all the answers on that first Father's Day but we began to talk and think about things we had not considered before.

Make family safety a priority and take the steps to reduce the risk of fires starting in your home. Involve everyone in planning how to get out in case of a fire. You probably won't have all of the answers, but at least you will have started the conversation.

Preventing fires in your home is important, and your family needs to know that they are important to you.

ACKNOWLEDGEMENTS

I would like to thank a number of people who encouraged me to learn about home safety and how to prevent fires.

I would like to thank everyone at Redfin, who supported my home inspection business when we were both just getting started. Their unconditional support helped me find my voice as a teacher in home maintenance and safety. I really enjoyed the times that I taught your staff about construction materials and your home buyers about the home inspection process.

I would like to thank the professional firefighters of Eastside Fire and Rescue in Issaquah, WA, who shared their knowledge and experience with me. Those moments helped me to respect the profession and show compassion for the community that we served.

I would like to thank Jay, Andrew, and Kevin from Station 79 in Maple Hills. You showed me how much of a family the fire department can be. You made countless nights of training and supporting the community the amazing experience that it was.

I would like to thank my editor, Mozelle Jordan, who helped make sure that what I wrote actually made sense.

I would like to thank my terrific illustrator, Michelle Bloemers. The images she created add so much to this story.

I would like to thank my children, Rachel, Jacob, and Reeve, who continue to amaze and inspire me every day. I always felt that if my kids had more opportunities and set higher goals than I did, then I would be a success. Well, they have made me feel more successful than I could ever have imagined.

I would especially like to thank my wife, Theresa, who encouraged me to make this project a reality. She supported me, challenged me, and calmed my fear. She taught me to recognize that there is always a solution to any obstacle.

And lastly, I want to thank every parent, grandparent, child, aunt, uncle, or family friend who has taken the time to read this book and made the safety of their loved ones a primary importance.

YEARLY MAINTENANCE SCHEDULE

Earlier in this book, we discussed the places around your home where fires are most likely to start, as well as the steps you can take to reduce the risk of fires starting.

Keeping up with fire safety is an ongoing effort, but by spreading these projects throughout the year, you can make them less of a chore and more of an organized, committed effort to protect your family.

January

• **Check air flow through the forced air heating systems.** Replace furnace filters every three months and keep furniture away from cold air returns to keep your system operating efficiently and safely.

February

• **Maintain garage separation from the interior spaces.** Proper fire barriers should be installed and maintained to prevent a garage fire from quickly moving inside or into other parts of the home. This includes covering any openings in the wall between the garage and the interior, as well as to the attic or crawl space. Additionally, the door between your garage and your interior should be fitted with self-closing hinges and free of any pet doors.

March

• **Check the age of smoke and CO alarms.** Replace older alarms with new combination, dual sensor alarms that will provide the best protection for both smoldering and flaming fires.
• **Change batteries and test smoke and carbon monoxide alarms twice a year.** If using older alarms, change the 9-volt or AA batteries twice a year but regardless of the battery life, test all alarms twice a year.

April

• **Check electrical service wires.** Confirm clearance of service wires from tree branches and other vegetation.
• **Clear fallen leaves and other debris from your roof and gutters.** This will reduce the risk of ignition and allow for proper drainage.
• **Clear vegetation from around hydrants in your neighborhood.**
• **Check air flow through the forced air heating systems.** To keep your system operating efficiently and safely, replace furnace filters every three months and keep furniture away from cold air returns.

May

• **Clear lint accumulation between the dryer and the exterior.** Vacuum out any lint accumulation within the appliance. Replace flexible ductwork between the appliance and the wall and clean the rigid metal ductwork between the interior wall and the exterior discharge. These steps reduce the risk of lint fires and improve the drying efficiency of the appliance.

June

• **Check age of fire extinguishers.** These units have a lifespan of up to 10 years. To determine the date of manufacture for your extinguishers, check the manufacturer's website to translate a code stamped on the unit. Replace if approaching ten years or older.
• **Check extinguisher gauges for proper charge.** If not in the green, extinguishers should be replaced.
• **Check safety items beside your bed.** Change the batteries in the flashlight, and confirm other items are accessible.
• **Check secondary pathways, and make sure all windows can be opened.** Trim any vegetation and clear obstacles between the window and the front yard.
• **Create and practice your Father's Day Fire Plan.**

YEARLY MAINTENANCE SCHEDULE

July

• **Check gas appliance shutoffs.** Operate the valve on gas shutoffs, for every gas appliance, to ensure they have not seized up.

• **Check air flow through the forced air heating systems.** Replace furnace filters every three months and keep furniture away from cold air returns, to keep your system operating efficiently and safely.

August

• **Have the fireplace and chimney inspected and cleaned yearly, by a qualified chimney sweep.** Chimney sweeps will eliminate any accumulated creosote, clear any blockages, evaluate and repair any structural weakness, and ensure proper and safe operation. The Chimney Safety Institute of America provides further information regarding fireplace and chimney maintenance, including how to find a qualified chimney sweep in your area.

• **Install or check chimney caps.** Also called spark arrestors, these devices prevent burning embers from escaping to the exterior and can prevent animals from entering the chimney flue. If missing or damaged, they should be replaced. These can be installed by a competent homeowner, a handyman, or a chimney sweep. Care should always be exercised when walking on roofs or working on ladders.

September

• **Check electrical service wires.** Confirm clearance of service wires from tree branches and other vegetation.

• **Check the age of smoke and CO alarms.** Replace older alarms with new combination, dual sensor alarms to provide the best protection for both smoldering and flaming fires.

• **Change batteries and test smoke and carbon monoxide alarms twice a year.** If using older alarms, change the 9-volt or AA batteries twice a year but regardless of the battery life, test all alarms twice a year.

96

October

• **Service your heating systems every year.** Proper maintenance of fuel, combustion air, and venting are the key components of proper and safe operation. When improper, there is an increased risk of toxic gas exposure and fire. Improper combustion, due to debris accumulation on the burners or limited combustion air, increases the risk of carbon monoxide production. Failure of the heat exchanger, which is the primary barrier between the flame and the room air, also increases the risk of carbon monoxide production. Improper or failed venting of these systems, to the exterior, can also increase the risk of toxic gases entering the interior of the home. All of these factors can be assessed and reduced with annual inspection, service, and cleaning by a qualified, licensed heating contractor.

• **Check air flow through the forced air heating systems.** Replace furnace filters every three months and keep furniture away from cold air returns, to keep your system operating efficiently and safely.

November

• **Clear fallen leaves and other debris from your roof and gutters.** This will reduce the risk of ignition and allow for proper drainage.

December

• **Have a qualified, licensed electrician inspect electrical panels, switches, outlets, and visible wiring for damage or overheating.** Because assessment of these symptoms may only be possible behind outlet and switch cover plates or behind the cover of the main electrical panel, this should only be completed by a qualified professional.

ADDITIONAL RESOURCES

National Fire Protection Association (NFPA)
www.nfpa.org

Federal Emergency Management Administration (FEMA)
www.fema.gov

Consumer Product Safety Commission
www.cpsc.gov

Chimney Sweep Institute of America
www.csia.org

American Red Cross
www.redcross.org

American Cancer Society
www.cancer.org

Close Before You Doze
www.closeyourdoor.org

CalFire, Wildfire Information
www.readyforwildfire.org

Father's Day Fire Plan
www.fathersdayfireplan.com

SOURCES

[1] Hall, J. R. (2011). *Fatal Effects of Fire.* Quincy, MA: National Fire Protection Association.

[2,3] Kerber, S. (2012). *Analysis of Changing Residential Fire Dynamics and its Implications on Firefighter Operational Timeframes.* Underwriters Laboratories.

[4] Kuligowski, E. (2009). *The Process of Human Behavior in Fires.* National Institute of Standards and Technology.

[5] Duval, R. F. (2006). *NFPA Case Study: Nightclub Fires.* Quincy, MA: National Fire Protection Association.

[6] Campbell, R. (2019). *Home Electrical Fires.* Quincy, MA: National Fire Protection Association.

[7] Campbell, R. (2017). *Home Fires Involving Clothes Dryers and Washing Machines.* Quincy, MA: National Fire Protection Association.

[8] Ahrens, M. (2019). *Home Fires Started by Smoking.* Quincy, MA: National Fire Protection Association.

[9] Ahrens, M. (2019). *Smoke Alarms in U.S. Home Fires.* National Fire Protection Association.

[10] UL Firefighter Safety Research Institute. (2018, October 05). *Close Before You Doze.* From UL Firefighter Safety Research Institute: https://ulfirefightersafety.org/research-projects/close-your-door.html

[11,12] National Fire Protection Association. (2016). *Home Fire Sprinklers.* From NFPA Public Education Division: https://www.nfpa.org/-/media/Files/Public-Education/Resources/Safety-tip-sheets/Home_Sprinklers.pdf

About the Author

Robert Wittenberg is a former ASHI Certified Home Inspector, having performed nearly 3,000 home inspections in Washington State and California. He is also a former Volunteer Firefighter and EMT in Washington State. But most of all, he is a husband and father of three. He started Father's Day Fire Plan because he believes taking simple steps can help keep families safe in the event of a fire.

About the Illustrator

Michelle Bloemers was born and raised in Brighton, Michigan. She earned her undergraduate degree from Michigan State University in 2015 and moved out to Oregon with her husband, Jonathan, and their dog, Elliot, in 2016. She has been drawing and painting her entire life but is now studying to become a dentist at Oregon Health & Science University School of Dentistry in Portland. In her spare time, Michelle enjoys creating art and sewing, as well as hiking and running.

Made in the USA
Monee, IL
01 July 2020

35511242R00064